Cooking with Edible Flowers

Miriam Jacobs

CONTENTS

Introduction

Eating flowers planted and cared for by your own hands is one of the many joys of being a gardener. Edible flowers are more than just beautiful garnishes for your dishes; they add flavors, textures, and aromas that no other food category can mimic.

Cookbook writers face an interesting challenge. The flavors of some foods vary widely depending on the season, the growing conditions, and other factors. Just imagine the texture and flavor of a freshly picked summer tomato compared to those of a cold, hard-as-a-baseball supermarket tomato in winter! This same variability occurs when cooking with flowers. The flavor and color of two rose petals can be very different, and therefore a recipe using rose petals will never come out exactly the same way twice. Similarly, the flavor of a chive blossom can be anywhere from slightly oniony to quite sharp, depending on soil conditions, hours of sunlight, and so on. While this variety adds a lot of excitement to flower cooking, it is always something to keep in mind. Use a light touch when you start out; when you get to know flowers from your own garden, you will be able to adjust the recipes to your taste.

Commonsense Cautions

Because edible flowers are new to many people, it's important to point out some safety issues. The most obvious one is that not all flowers are edible; in fact, quite a few are poisonous. *Eat only those flowers you are positive you can identify.* Do not experiment on your own; if you're unsure whether a flower is edible, don't add it to the menu until you've confirmed with an expert — a horticulturalist, a reference guide, or a nursery owner, for example — that it's safe to eat. In addition, if you have asthma or allergies, you will want to be just as cautious with edible flowers as you would be with other foods.

There's another "rule" when it comes to eating flowers: Eat them only if you are positive that they have been grown organically. Never eat flowers picked at the side of the road; they are polluted by automobile emissions. You should avoid flowers from a nursery as well; they most likely will have been sprayed with pesticides. Don't forget: Because flowers are not usually considered a food, they are likely to be sprayed with stuff you absolutely should not ingest. Pick them in your own garden (if you garden organically), find a nursery or herb shop that offers organically grown flowers, or get them from trusted friends with organic gardens.

The Best Blossoms for Eating

If your only criterion is that they be nonpoisonous, then many flowers are edible — but not all of them are yummy. In this bulletin I've provided an overview of the best-known, most delicious edible flowers. I've included recipes here for the flowers of the following plants, which are among the easiest to identify:

- Basil
- Chamomile
- Chives
- Dill
- Hibiscus
- Lavender
- Marigolds
- Nasturtiums
- Roses
- Violas (pansies, Johnny-jump-ups, and violets)

Once you've prepared some of the recipes in this booklet, you'll be ready to experiment with other flowers. Again, be sure you can identify them! Try cooking with the blossoms of some of the following plants:

- Bee balm
- Borage
- Dandelion
- Daylily
- Fennel
- Honeysuckle
- Marjoram
- Mint
- Oregano
- Rosemary
- Thyme
- Yucca

Preparing Flowers for the Dinner Table

Flowers are among the most delicate of foods, and they need special care. Before you can eat or process flowers, you first need to wash them. Because of their fragile nature, the best method of washing is simply to rinse them quickly in cold water and gently shake off the remaining drops of water.

Fresh flowers don't keep particularly well, so it is best to use them freshly picked. If this isn't practical for you, you can also harvest them with their stems and place them in a vase with some water, just as you might do with any bouquet.

You can also dry flowers to save them for later use. Use a commercial dehydrator, if you have one, or simply place the blossoms on paper towels, where they will be dry in a day or two. Long-stemmed flowers can be hung to dry from racks, much like herbs. Store the dried flowers in airtight containers in a cool, dark location. As with all dried produce, be sure that the flowers are thoroughly dry before you pack them away, as excess moisture can cause mold to form.

The Best Dressings

The simplest way to use edible flowers is in salads. When doing so, be sure to use a mild dressing to avoid drowning out the flowers' delicate flavors. Serve the dressing on the side; pouring dressing over the flowers will quickly discolor them.

MUMU'S SWEET DRESSING

My mom made the following sweet dressing for fruit salads. Try it on salads that include roses, violets, pansies, or lavender.

>   ¾ cup (177 ml) mild-flavored vegetable oil,
>   such as safflower
>   ⅓ cup (79 ml) honey
>   ¼ cup (59 ml) freshly squeezed lemon juice

Place all ingredients in a blender and blend for 10 seconds. Any leftovers should be refrigerated and will keep for 1 week.

MAKES 1⅓ CUPS (316 ML)

SAVORY SALAD DRESSING

For more savory salads, which might include basil flowers, nasturtium, and dill flowers, try this basic dressing.

¾ cup (177 ml) extra-virgin olive oil
¼ cup (59 ml) balsamic vinegar
1 tablespoon (15 ml) Dijon-style mustard
¼ teaspoon (1.3 ml) salt
¼ teaspoon (1.3 ml) freshly ground black pepper

Place all ingredients in a blender and blend for 10 seconds. Any leftovers should be refrigerated and will keep for 2 weeks.

MAKES 1 CUP (237 ML)

Basil Flowers

I used to feel guilty when my basil bolted. But then I learned that you can eat the flowers! Basil flowers taste a little like the leaves and therefore make a great addition to any dish in which you use basil, such as pasta or pizza.

BASIL FLOWER SALAD

This unusual salad is easy to make and adds a touch of class to any dining table.

1 small head romaine lettuce
1 avocado
¼ cup (59 ml) freshly grated Parmesan cheese
A handful of basil flowers
Oil-and-vinegar dressing

1. Wash the lettuce and tear the leaves into bite-size pieces. Place the lettuce in a serving bowl.

2. Peel and pit the avocado and cut it into bite-size pieces. Sprinkle the avocado pieces over the lettuce, then sprinkle Parmesan cheese over all.

3. Sprinkle basil flowers over the salad. Serve immediately, with dressing on the side.

MAKES 4 SERVINGS

BASIL FLOWER FRITTERS

The idea for this recipe began when I attempted to batter-fry daylilies, but the result was bland. Then I tried nasturtium flowers, thinking their peppery taste would come through, but again I was disappointed. But while I was in the garden I picked a stalk of basil flowers, and when I batter-fried them, they were nothing short of spectacular! You can even use the basil stalk when the flowers have fallen off.

Serve a few fritters per person as an appetizer and watch everybody's eyes light up. You can also batter-dip and fry parsley at the same time. This recipe is also a great way to use up flat beer!

⅔ cup (158 ml) flour
½ teaspoon (2.5 ml) salt, plus a pinch more if desired
¼ teaspoon (1.3 ml) freshly ground black pepper
A pinch of ground cayenne pepper (optional)
1 egg yolk
⅓–½ cup (79–118 ml) beer (or nonalcoholic beer)
Vegetable oil, for frying
12 basil flower stalks

1. Line a plate with a double thickness of paper towels. In a small bowl, combine the flour, salt, black pepper, and cayenne. Add the egg yolk; mix until well blended.

2. The amount of beer to add depends on the humidity in the room. Add a little beer, whisking constantly; continue adding beer until the mixture is the consistency of thick pancake batter.

3. Fill a deep frying pan (or any thick-bottomed pan) with about 2 inches (5 cm) of oil. Set over high heat. Drop a little bit of batter into the oil and watch it carefully; when the batter starts to brown, reduce the heat to medium. Pick up a basil flower stalk by the stem and swish it in the batter, making sure to coat the whole stalk except the part you are holding.

4. Place the batter-covered stalks into the hot oil, a few at a time. Fry until brown on both sides, turning once. (Take extreme care to keep your hands and forearms well away from the spattering of hot oil!)

5. Transfer the fritters to the paper towel–lined plate. Sprinkle with salt if you like; serve immediately.

MAKES 12 FRITTERS

TOMATO PESTO SOUP

This cold, fragrant, garlicky soup is perfect on a hot day. Make the tomato base early in the morning, when you won't mind having the stove on for a few minutes. Let the base cool in the refrigerator all day, and in the evening you can have delicious soup in 5 minutes.

  2 **tablespoons (30 ml) extra-virgin olive oil**
  1 **medium onion, chopped**
  2 **cloves garlic, chopped, plus 1 whole clove**
  2 **pounds (908 g) very ripe tomatoes (about 6 medium tomatoes), chopped**
  1 **cup (237 ml) loosely packed basil leaves**
  1 **tablespoon (15 ml) lemon juice**
  ¼ **cup (59 ml) freshly grated Parmesan cheese**
    A handful of basil flowers

1. Heat the oil in a large frying pan over medium-high. Add the onion; sauté until soft. Add the chopped garlic; sauté for 1 minute longer. Add the tomatoes; cook the mixture, uncovered, until the tomatoes are soft, about 15 minutes. Remove from heat and let stand until cool; then chill until serving time.

2. Place the basil leaves, lemon juice, and whole garlic clove in a blender. Add the chilled tomato mixture; blend well.

3. Pour the soup into individual soup bowls. Sprinkle each serving with Parmesan cheese and basil flowers. Serve cold.

MAKES 4 SERVINGS

FRESH TOMATO SAUCE

This homemade fresh pasta sauce hands-down wins out over the processed and preserved canned sauces of the grocery store.

2 **pounds (908 g) ripe tomatoes (about 6 medium tomatoes)**
2 **tablespoons (30 ml) extra-virgin olive oil**
1 **onion, chopped**
2 **cloves garlic, minced**
¼ **cup (59 ml) loosely packed basil leaves**
1 **cup (237 ml) basil flowers**
Salt and freshly ground black pepper

1. With a sharp knife, make a shallow cross-shaped cut in the bottom of each tomato.

2. Bring a large pot of water to a boil. Turn off the heat and drop the tomatoes into the water. Let stand for a few minutes, until the skin looks loose. Remove the tomatoes from the water; let stand until slightly cooled. Peel off the skins and discard; coarsely chop the tomatoes, reserving any juice.

3. Heat the oil in a medium saucepan over medium-high. Add the onion; sauté until translucent. Add the garlic; cook for 1 minute more. Add the tomatoes and any juice; cook for 5 minutes. Remove from heat; let stand until slightly cooled.

4. Pour the tomato mixture into a food processor fitted with a metal blade; add the basil leaves. (You might have to do this in several batches.) Process the sauce to the desired thickness; you can make it completely smooth or leave it slightly chunky if you prefer. Return the sauce to the saucepan and season to taste with salt and pepper; heat to serving temperature.

5. To serve, pour the sauce over cooked pasta; sprinkle with basil flowers.

MAKES ENOUGH SAUCE FOR 4–6 SERVINGS OF PASTA

Chamomile

Chamomile is such a pretty perennial to grow, and sipping chamomile tea on a cold winter's day takes you back to the warmth of summer.

To dry chamomile flowers, pick them and lay them on a clean cloth or screen to dry in the sun. If they are not dry by the end of the day, finish drying them in the oven on very low heat. When the blossoms are thoroughly dry, store them in an airtight container.

CHAMOMILE TEA

This is a very soothing tea, great after a stressful day.

- 1   **cup (237 ml) boiling water**
- 1   **teaspoon (5 ml) dried chamomile flowers**
- 1   **teaspoon (5 ml) honey or 1 lemon slice**

1. Pour the boiling water into a teapot. Add the chamomile flowers; let steep for about 5 minutes

2. Pour the tea through a sieve into a cup. Serve immediately with honey or a slice of lemon.

MAKES 1 SERVING

Chive Blossoms

Chive blossoms are usually the first edible flowers to bloom in my garden, and they do so without any help from me. The strength of their flavor varies widely, so taste them before using them in a recipe. To use chive blossoms, cut the purple florets off the stem or simply pull them off in bunches.

COLD YOGURT, CUCUMBER, AND CHIVE BLOSSOM SOUP

This is a fabulous soup to make when it's just too hot to cook but you want to prepare something special. For a more filling soup, add cold cooked and peeled shrimp.

- 2 cups (473 ml) plain yogurt
- ½ cup (118 ml) walnut halves
- 2 cloves garlic, minced
- ½ teaspoon (2. 5 ml) salt
- 1 large cucumber, peeled
- 6 chive blossoms, divided

1. In a food processor fitted with a steel blade, combine the yogurt, walnuts, garlic, and salt. Process until the walnuts are completely ground.

2. Pour the yogurt mixture into a bowl; set aside. Replace the food processor bowl (you do not have to wash it first). Fit the food processor with a coarse grating blade. Grate the cucumber.

3. Add the grated cucumber to the yogurt mixture; stir well. Chill until serving time.

4. Pour the soup into serving bowls. Remove the flowers from two of the chive blossoms and sprinkle them over the soup. Float the remaining whole chive blossoms on the soup as a garnish.

MAKES 4 SERVINGS

HOME FRIES WITH CHIVE BLOSSOMS

Home fries is a classic leftover dish; it's what I always do with leftover boiled or steamed potatoes. Chive flowers upgrade this staple to elegant weekend brunch fare.

¼ cup (59 ml) extra-virgin olive oil
4 cups (946 ml) boiled or steamed potatoes, sliced
Salt and freshly ground black pepper
8 chive blossoms, florets snipped off and separated

1. Heat the oil in a heavy-bottomed frying pan over high.

2. Add the potato slices; cook until the bottoms begin to brown. Using a large spatula, turn the potatoes; sprinkle with salt and pepper to taste. Sprinkle with chive florets.

3. Continue cooking until the bottom is brown. Serve immediately.

MAKES 4 SERVINGS

CHIVE VINAIGRETTE

This recipe comes from my friend Joel Goodman, who also gave me some of his abundant chive blossoms to make it with. Be a little patient while adding the oil, and you will have a rosy dressing that is creamy, sweet, sour, and oniony all at the same time.

¼ cup (59 ml) lemon juice
¼ cup (59 ml) rice vinegar
1 tablespoon (15 ml) honey
8 chive blossoms, florets snipped off and separated
1 small clove garlic
1 cup (237 ml) extra-virgin olive oil
Salt and freshly ground black pepper

1. In a blender, combine the lemon juice, vinegar, honey, chive blossoms, and garlic. Blend until the blossoms are thoroughly liquefied.

2. With the blender running, add the oil a little at a time, blending completely after each addition, until all the oil is in and emulsified. Season with salt and pepper to taste. If you're not going to use the dressing right away, cover and refrigerate; it will keep for 1 day.

MAKES 1 CUP (237 ML)

Dill Flowers

Dill flowers taste like a combination of dill and anise. They're a great way to decorate dishes flavored with dill: Floating dill flowers in vichyssoise, for instance, is a pretty and delicious presentation.

DILLED BEET SALAD

The beets tint this salad a pretty pink. This is a wonderful year-round salad: It's great cold in the summer and a delicious way to eat your root vegetables in the winter. To turn it into a meal, add 1 cup (237 ml) of diced, fully cooked ham.

- 2   beets, peeled
- 3   medium potatoes, boiled and diced
- 3   hard-cooked eggs, chopped
- 2   medium Granny Smith apples, diced
- ¼   cup (59 ml) minced onion
- ½   cup (118 ml) mayonnaise
- 1   teaspoon (5 ml) apple cider vinegar
- ¼   teaspoon (1.3 ml) salt
- ¼   teaspoon (1.3 ml) freshly ground black pepper
- 2   tablespoons (30 ml) dill flowers

1. Grate the beets in a food processor or by hand. In a large bowl, combine the grated beets, potatoes, eggs, apples, and onion.

2. In a small bowl, combine the mayonnaise, vinegar, salt, and pepper.

3. Pour the dressing over the beet-potato mixture and toss well. Sprinkle with dill flowers. Serve immediately or chill first.

MAKES 4 SERVINGS

DILLED SWEET POTATO

This recipe is for one very hungry person, and that is how it developed: I was famished and wanted something filling and satisfying. Of course you can double or quadruple the recipe if you're feeding others!

1   large sweet potato, peeled and cut in chunks
2   cloves garlic
¼   cup (59 ml) chopped pecans
1   tablespoon (15 ml) extra-virgin olive oil
1   teaspoon (5 ml) butter
1   teaspoon (5 ml) sweet miso
3   dill flowers

1. Fill a large pot with about 1 inch of water. Bring to a boil. Place the sweet potato and garlic in a steamer basket and place in the pot, over the boiling water. Cover and let steam until the potato is tender.

2. Mash the sweet potato and garlic. Add the pecans, oil, butter, and miso; mix well.

3. Sprinkle the dill flowers over the potato mixture; serve immediately.

MAKES 1 SERVING

CUCUMBER–DILL FLOWER SALAD

Dill and cucumber is a classic combination; adding dill flowers gives the salad a fresh twist.

1   medium cucumber
2   teaspoons (10 ml) salt
2   tablespoons (30 ml) apple cider vinegar
1   tablespoon (15 ml) sesame seeds
1   tablespoon (15 ml) dill flowers

1. Peel and thinly slice the cucumber. Sprinkle the salt over the cucumber slices and rub it into the surfaces. Place the cucumber slices in a colander and let drain for about an hour.

2. Using your hands or the back of a spoon, press any remaining moisture out of the cucumber. Transfer the slices to a serving bowl.

3. Sprinkle the cucumber slices with vinegar; toss to coat. Sprinkle with sesame seeds and dill flowers. Serve cold.

MAKES 3 OR 4 SERVINGS

DILL POTATO SALAD

Potato salad is a summertime must. Here the dill flowers add visual appeal and a subtly different layer of dill flavor.

6–8 new potatoes, diced
  1 chive (white part only), minced
  ⅓ cup (79 ml) mayonnaise
  ⅓ cup (79 ml) chopped pimento-stuffed olives
  1 tablespoon (15 ml) minced fresh dill
  1 teaspoon (5 ml) Dijon-style mustard
  ½ teaspoon (2.5 ml) salt
  4 dill flowers, flowers only
  3 dill flowers stalks, for decoration

1. Fill a large pot with about 1 inch (2.5 cm) of water. Bring to a boil. Place the potatoes in a steamer basket and place in the pot, over the boiling water. Cover and let steam until the potatoes are tender.

2. In a medium bowl, combine the chive, mayonnaise, olives, dill, mustard, salt, and the four dill flowers. Add the warm potatoes to the dressing and toss to coat. Let stand until cool.

3. Spoon the potato salad into a serving bowl and decorate with the flower stalks. Serve immediately.

MAKES 4 SERVINGS

Hibiscus

I do not have hibiscus in my garden, but I can buy the dried flowers at my local herb shop. If you do grow this pretty flower, by all means dry the red petals yourself.

HIBISCUS TEA

This dramatic-looking red tea is very fresh and tart.

> 1 teaspoon (5 ml) dried hibiscus flowers
> 1 cup (237 ml) boiling water
> Honey

1. Place the dried hibiscus flowers in a warm teapot. Pour the boiling water over the flowers; let steep for 1 minute.

2. Pour the tea through a sieve into a cup. Sweeten with honey to taste; serve immediately.

MAKES 1 SERVING

ICED HIBISCUS TEA

This cool, refreshing tea makes a wonderful summertime treat.

> 1½ teaspoons (7.5 ml) dried hibiscus flowers
> 1 cup (237 ml) boiling water
> Honey
> 1 slice lemon

1. Place the dried hibiscus flowers in a warm teapot. Pour boiling water over the flowers; let steep for 1 minute.

2. Pour the tea through a sieve. Sweeten with honey to taste. Chill the tea until cold.

3. When the tea is cold, strain it again and pour it over ice cubes. Add a lemon slice; serve immediately.

MAKES 1 SERVING

PINK HIBISCUS RICE

This rice dish has a most unusual pink-purple color. The hibiscus gives the rice a slight tartness, while the currants make it sweet.

1   cup (237 ml) uncooked basmati rice
2   cups (473 ml) water
2   teaspoons (10 ml) dried hibiscus flowers
⅓   cup (79 ml) dried currants
¼   teaspoon (1.3 ml) salt
Fresh hibiscus flowers (optional)

1. Place the basmati rice in a colander and rinse under running water until the water runs clear.

2. Place the water in a saucepan; add the dried hibiscus flowers. Bring the water to a rolling boil over high heat; add the rice, currants, and salt. Stir once; when the water returns to a boil, cover the pan and reduce the heat to very low. Simmer the rice mixture for 20 minutes.

3. Fluff the rice; serve immediately. Top with hibiscus flowers, if desired.

MAKES 3 OR 4 SERVINGS

HIBISCUS STRAWBERRIES

The tart flavor and deep red color of hibiscus tea go perfectly with strawberries. Make this beautiful fruit salad in a clear glass bowl so you can really appreciate the vivid color.

1   tablespoon (15 ml) dried hibiscus flowers
½   cup (118 ml) boiling water
1   tablespoon (15 ml) honey
1   pint (473 ml) fresh strawberries, hulled, divided

1. Place the hibiscus flowers in a bowl; pour the boiling water over them. Let steep for 3 minutes.

2. Pour the tea through a sieve into a bowl or glass measuring cup. Add the honey; stir well. Let stand until cool.

3. Transfer the tea to a blender; add ⅔ cup (158 ml) of the strawberries. Blend until smooth.

4. Slice the remaining strawberries. Pour the hibiscus-strawberry sauce over the sliced berries, then chill for 1 hour. Serve cold.

MAKES 3 OR 4 SERVINGS

Lavender

The somewhat floppy, gray-green lavender leaves and long spikes of purple flowers create a soft corner in the garden. You can use the entire spike for decorating or for flavoring (try cooking it in milk for an unusual and delicious beverage!). However, for flavoring sugars and more delicate decorative concoctions, use only the small purple flowers.

LAVENDER CUSTARD

This easy-to-make custard is redolent with the delicate fragrance of lavender blossoms.

- 4 cups (946 ml) milk, divided
- 5 lavender spikes, divided
- 5 eggs, beaten
- 1 cup (237 ml) sugar
- 1 tablespoon (15 ml) vanilla extract
- A pinch of salt

1. Preheat the oven to 350°F (177°C). In a double boiler set over simmering water, combine 1 cup (237 ml) of the milk and three lavender spikes; cook, without boiling, for 10 minutes.

2. Pour the lavender-scented milk through a sieve into a large bowl. Whisk in the remaining milk. Add the eggs, sugar, vanilla, and salt; whisk well. Pour the mixture into a large, ovenproof, ceramic mold.

3. Stand the mold in a roasting pan. Carefully pour water into the roasting pan until it reaches a depth of about 2 inches (5 cm).

4. Bake the custard until a wooden skewer inserted in the center comes out clean, about 1 hour. Let stand until cooled to room temperature; if you're not going to eat it right away, keep it refrigerated.

5. To serve, loosen the edges with a knife and invert the custard onto a serving platter. Decorate with the flowers from the remaining lavender sprigs.

MAKES 4 SERVINGS

HERBES DE PROVENCE

This is a great holiday gift to make for friends and family, so be sure to dry extra lavender when your crop comes in. Add a tag with a recipe for the herb mixture.

¼ cup (59 ml) dried thyme
3 tablespoons (45 ml) dried marjoram
2 tablespoons (30 ml) dried summer savory
1 teaspoon (5 ml) dried rosemary
½ teaspoon (2.5 ml) dried sage
½ teaspoon (2.5 ml) dried lavender flowers

Combine all the ingredients and store in an airtight jar. Crush the herbs between your fingers before adding them to food.

MAKES ABOUT ⅔ CUP (158 ML)

LAVENDER SUGAR

During the past 10 years or so, people have become enamored with flavored oils, vinegars, and sugars because of the instant taste boost they deliver to dishes. It's not a new trick, though: Keeping a piece of vanilla bean in the sugar bowl is an age-old tradition.

Keep in mind that most flavored sugars have a very mellow taste that won't stand up to strongly flavored dishes. Use your lavender sugar to add a subtle new flavor to mild foods such as vanilla icing and chamomile tea.

¼ cup (59 ml) lavender flowers
1 cup (237 ml) granulated sugar

1. Dry the lavender flowers completely.

2. Alternate the sugar and flowers in several layers in an airtight container. Let stand for at least 2 weeks.

3. Sift the sugar to remove the flowers; store the sugar in an airtight container.

Variation: You can also make this with beautiful bits of lavender in the sugar. Combine the dried flowers and sugar in a food processor and process until the lavender is finely ground. (You can also pulverize the lavender in a coffee or spice grinder and then add it to the sugar, but be sure the grinder is very clean first. Otherwise, the lavender will pick up whatever flavors might linger.)

MAKES ABOUT 1 CUP (237 ML)

FROSTED LAVENDER STICKS

Excerpted from *Herbal Sweets,*
by Ruth Bass (Storey Books, 1996)

Sugared, lavender flowers are a crisp, pretty nibble. For variety, substitute violets or rose petals for the lavender.

12 stalks fresh lavender flowers
1   egg white, beaten until frothy
½ cup (118 ml) granulated sugar

1. Dip the flowers of the lavender stalks in egg white, then roll in or dust with sugar. If you are worried about eating uncooked egg whites, substitute the proper amount of pasteurized, dried egg whites.

2. Air-dry on waxed paper

MAKES 1 DOZEN STICKS

SWORDFISH STEAK EN PROVENCE

With a jar of Herbes de Provence (at left) in your pantry, you're about 20 minutes away from this incredibly flavorful seafood dish. Serve the swordfish with steamed potatoes and carrots for a fast, delicious meal.

Flour for dredging
Salt and freshly ground black pepper
1   2-inch-thick (5 cm) swordfish steak (about 1 pound; 454 g)
1   teaspoon (5 ml) Herbes de Provence
5   tablespoons (75 ml) butter
¼ cup (59 ml) white wine

1. In a shallow bowl, combine the flour, salt, and pepper. Dredge the fish steak in the flour.

2. Press the herb mixture into the surface of the fish.

3. Melt the butter in a large skillet over medium heat; add the fish. Cook the fish for about 8 minutes, then turn it over.

4. Continue to cook for another 7 or 8 minutes, until the fish flakes easily when tested with a fork.

5. Transfer the fish to a warmed platter. Add the wine to the pan and turn the heat to high; cook until the liquid is boiling, scraping the pan to incorporate any remaining bits of fish. Pour the sauce over the fish and serve immediately.

MAKES ABOUT 4 SERVINGS

Marigolds

I've raised easy-to-grow potted marigolds for years, but I had no idea until recently that their flowers are edible! You eat only the petals, which are slightly bitter, but they are a great addition to salads and the following recipes.

MARIGOLD PILAF

Marigolds add lovely yellow specks to this fragrant rice dish.

- 2 tablespoons (30 ml) butter
- ¼ cup (59 ml) diced onion
- 1 cup (237 ml) uncooked white rice
- 1 clove garlic, minced
- ½ teaspoon (2.5 ml) salt
- 2 cups (473 ml) water
- ¼ cup (59 ml) raisins
- 3 tablespoons (45 ml) minced marigold petals
- 1 whole marigold

1. Melt the butter in a heavy saucepan over medium-high heat. Add the onion and sauté until transparent. Add the rice, garlic, and salt; mix well until all the rice is covered with butter.

2. Add the water, raisins, and minced marigolds; bring to a boil. Cover the pan, reduce the heat to low, and simmer for 20 minutes.

3. Fluff the rice and transfer it to a serving bowl. Carefully tear the petals from the remaining flower and sprinkle them over the rice. Serve immediately.

MAKES 3 OR 4 SERVINGS

Nasturtiums

Nasturtiums provide multiple pleasures: They are easy to grow, they have lovely bright flowers, and both the flowers and leaves are edible!

SAUSAGE AND PEPPERS
WITH NASTURTIUM BLOSSOMS

This classic mix is equally tasty spooned over steaming hot pasta and scooped onto crusty French bread. Since this dish reheats very well, make it while the day is still cool and then simply warm it up for a hearty and flavorful supper.

2 tablespoons (30 ml) extra-virgin olive oil
1 onion, sliced, rings separated
2 cloves garlic, minced
1 red bell pepper, cored and cut into strips
1 green bell pepper, cored and cut into strips
Salt and freshly ground black pepper
1 pound (454 g) link-style chicken sausage, fully cooked,
    cut into 1-inch (2.5 cm) pieces
¼ cup (59 ml) white wine
¼ cup (59 ml) freshly grated Parmesan cheese
1 cup (237 ml) nasturtium blossom petals

1. Heat the oil in a large frying pan over medium-high. Add the onions; sauté until they start to turn brown. Add the garlic; cook for 1 minute longer. Add the peppers; cook, stirring often, until the peppers wilt. Add salt and pepper to taste.

2. Add the sausage and wine to the pan. Cover and cook until the sausage is heated through, about 8 minutes.

3. Spoon the sausage and peppers into a serving bowl or over cooked pasta. Sprinkle with Parmesan cheese and nasturtium petals. Serve immediately.

MAKES 4 SERVINGS

NASTURTIUM SALAD
WITH MARIGOLD-PETAL DRESSING

This lovely salad uses both the leaves and the flowers of this versatile plant.

For the dressing:
- 1 cup (237 ml) extra-virgin olive oil
- ¼ cup (59 ml) apple cider vinegar
- 1 tablespoon (15 ml) Dijon mustard
- ¼ cup (59 ml) marigold blossom petals, minced

For the salad:
- 4 cups (946 ml) mesclun salad mix
- 1 cup (237 ml) nasturtium leaves
- A handful of nasturtium blossom petals
- Marigold petals

Making the Dressing

Whisk together the oil, vinegar, and mustard, then stir in the marigold petals.

Making the Salad

1. Wash and thoroughly dry the salad mix. Line the salad bowl with the nasturtium leaves and place the salad mix in the center.

2. Sprinkle the nasturtium and marigold petals over the salad. Serve the salad with the Marigold-petal Dressing on the side.

MAKES 4 SERVINGS

Roses

They are the most romantic of flowers, their fragrance has been made into perfumes since biblical times, and they come in the most astonishing variety of colors! Experiment with the roses in your garden to discover which are the most flavorful. Since fragrance and flavor are so closely linked, traditional nonhybridized roses probably provide the most flavor.

Don't be tempted to make a rose-flavored dish from that gift of a perfect dozen roses: All commercially grown roses are heavily sprayed with non–food grade pesticides and fungicides and are definitely *not* for human consumption.

ROSE FINGER BOWL

One of the most elegant touches at a dinner party is a finger bowl of floating rose petals. It's especially thoughtful if the menu includes a dish that will be eaten with the fingers, such as whole artichokes. Simply set a small, shallow bowl at each place setting; fill the bowl with a few inches of water and float the rose petals on top. Be sure to set the table with cloth napkins so guests can dry their fingers after dipping them in the rose water.

ROSE STRAWBERRY JAM

This uncooked jam won't keep for very long, but it retains all the bouquet of fresh roses. To be sure you have a sweet jam, cut off all the white at the bottom of each rose petal. Rose water can be purchased in many specialty shops and Middle Eastern groceries.

- 3½ cups (828 ml) sugar
- 2 cups (473 ml) rose petals
- 1 cup (237 ml) fresh strawberries, washed and hulled
- 2 tablespoons (30 ml) rose water
- ¼ teaspoon (1.3 ml) orange extract
- ½ cup (118 ml) water
- 1 tablespoon (15 ml) lemon juice
- 1 package (3 ounces) liquid fruit pectin

1. Combine the sugar, rose petals, strawberries, rose water, and orange extract in a food processor fitted with a steel blade. Process, scraping down the sides several times, for 30 seconds.

2. In a small saucepan, combine the water, lemon juice, and pectin over high heat; bring to a boil. Boil the mixture for 3 minutes and then add it to the rose mixture in the food processor. Process until well mixed, about 30 seconds.

3. Pour as much jam as you will eat in the next month into clean jars. Pour the rest into freezer bags. Let jars and bags stand at room temperature overnight to set. Refrigerate the jam you will eat now and freeze the rest. (The frozen jam will keep for 2 to 3 months. Thaw as necessary.)

MAKES ABOUT 4 HALF-PINT JARS

RAS AL HANOUT

This spice mix can be used the way curry is used in Indian cooking; just like curry, its fragrance and flavor are nearly indescribable. It is the ground dried rose petals that make it so distinctly North African. Make this as a gift for special friends and add a recipe card so they'll know how to use it. Grind the cardamom, nutmeg, pepper, and coriander yourself if you can, but good-quality, store-bought spices will also give you amazing results.

>   1   **tablespoon (15 ml) cinnamon**
>   1   **teaspoon (5 ml) ground cardamom**
>   1   **teaspoon (5 ml) ground nutmeg**
>   1   **teaspoon (5 ml) ground cumin**
>   ½   **teaspoon (2.5 ml) freshly ground black pepper**
>   ¼   **teaspoon (1.3 ml) turmeric**
>   ¼   **teaspoon (1.3 ml) mace**
>   ¼   **teaspoon (1.3 ml) ground coriander**
>   1   **cup (237 ml) dried rose petals**

Sift together all of the spices to remove any little stems and pieces. Toss with the rose petals and store in an airtight jar.

MAKES ABOUT 1 CUP (237 ML)

ROSE AND LAVENDER FAIRYTALE TEA

The moment I made this whimsical tea, I wanted to drink it out of my childhood Bambi and Thumper china teacups. This is possibly the best tea to have with a small child, when you are pretending to be "real ladies." The tea has more aroma than flavor, but it is made for dunking vanilla cookies!

>   2   **tablespoons (30 ml) dried rose petals**
>   ½   **teaspoon (2.5 ml) dried lavender flowers**
>   2   **cups (473 ml) boiling water**
>   **Honey**

1. Place the rose petals and lavender flowers in a warm teapot. Pour the boiling water over the flowers and petals.

2. Let steep for 3 minutes. Pour the tea through a sieve into cups. Sweeten with honey to taste.

MAKES 2 SERVINGS

PERSIAN LAMB AND SPINACH STEW

This dish is my fantasy; it is possible that no person of Persian descent has ever cooked or eaten it! But the flavors and aromas sent me right to Scheherazade's tales. Serve this stew with Marigold Pilaf (see page 20) and pita bread.

    2 tablespoons (30 ml) flour
    2 tablespoons (30 ml) Ras al Hanout (at left)
    ½ teaspoon (2.5 ml) salt
    2 pounds (908 g) shoulder blade lamb chops
    1 tablespoon (15 ml) extra-virgin olive oil
    4 cloves garlic, minced
    4 scallions, chopped
    2 cups (473 ml) water
    1 10-ounce (292 g) package frozen spinach
    Juice of ½ lemon
    4 cups (946 ml) hot cooked white rice
    1 cup (237 ml) plain yogurt (optional)

1. In a shallow bowl, combine the flour, Ras al Hanout, and salt. Dredge the lamb chops in the flour mixture; reserve the leftover flour mixture.

2. Heat the oil in a deep frying pan over medium-high. Add the lamb; brown on all sides (you may have to do this in two batches).

3. Add the garlic and scallions; sauté for 1 minute. Sprinkle the reserved seasoned flour over the mixture in the pan; stir well. Carefully add the water (it might splatter a bit), spinach, and lemon juice; stirring and scraping the pan constantly, bring the stew to a boil. Reduce heat, cover, and simmer for 45 minutes, stirring occasionally.

4. Scoop the hot stew over rice. Top each serving with a dollop of yogurt if desired; serve immediately.

MAKES 4 SERVINGS

CHERRY CLAFOUTI WITH ROSE-FLAVORED ICE CREAM AND ROSE-SCENTED WHIPPED CREAM

Cherries and roses go together very well, and in this dessert they pair up in three different ways. Although this dish involves many steps, it is very easy to make. If you like it a lot, you'll want to get a cherry pitter: It makes pitting the cherries a breeze.

For the clafouti:
- 1½ pounds (681 g) fresh cherries, halved and pitted
- 3 eggs
- 1 cup (237 ml) milk
- ⅔ cup (158 ml) sugar
- ½ cup (118 ml) flour
- ¼ cup (59 ml) butter
- 2 teaspoons (30 ml) vanilla extract
- 1 teaspoon (5 ml) rose water

For the ice cream:
- 1 pint (473 ml) good-quality vanilla ice cream
- 2 tablespoons (30 ml) rose water

For the whipped cream:
- ½ cup (118 ml) whipping cream
- 1 tablespoon (15 ml) sugar
- 2 teaspoons (30 ml) rose water

Making the Clafouti

1. Preheat the oven to 400°F (204°C) and butter a casserole dish. Place the cherries in the casserole.

2. Combine the eggs, milk, sugar, flour, butter, vanilla, and rose water in a blender. Blend the batter until smooth; pour the batter over the cherries.

3. Bake the clafouti for 45 minutes. (*Note:* Because this cake has a custardlike center, a toothpick inserted in the center will not come out clean.)

Preparing the Ice Cream

1. Let the ice cream stand at room temperature until slightly softened.

2. Transfer the ice cream to a large bowl; add the rose water and beat with a stiff spatula until combined. Return the ice cream to the freezer.

Making the Whipped Cream

1. Pour the cream into a chilled bowl. Beat the cream with an electric mixer until it starts to thicken.

2. While beating constantly, add the sugar and then the rose water. Beat until stiff.

Serving the Clafouti

Scoop ice cream and whipped cream onto warm servings of clafouti; serve immediately.

MAKES 6 SERVINGS

NECTARINE–ROSE PETAL SALAD
WITH RASPBERRIES AND PINE NUTS

This salad is built on soft but deep flavors and scents. It's a special dish for a summer meal, served perhaps with a glass of sauterne, Kir, or simply raspberry iced tea.

2   cups (473 ml) Boston lettuce leaves, washed and dried
1   cup (237 ml) rose petals, divided
4   ripe apricots, halved and pitted
1   cup (237 ml) raspberries, divided
½ cup (118 ml) pine nuts
Mumu's Sweet Dressing (see page 4)

1. In a large bowl, toss together the lettuce and half of the rose petals.

2. Cut the apricot halves into slices. Place the apricot slices in the bowl. Sprinkle with ¾ cup (177 ml) raspberries and the pine nuts.

3. In a food processor or blender, combine the remaining raspberries with the salad dressing. Process until berries are pureed.

4. Sprinkle the remaining rose petals over the salad. Serve immediately, with the dressing on the side.

MAKES 4 SERVINGS

Violas

Pansies, Johnny-jump-ups, and violets (all members of the Viola family) tend not to have a pronounced taste, but they are so beautiful that they are a joy to cook with. Of the three, violets have the most flavor and fragrance.

HONEYED STARFRUIT, PEACH, AND PANSY SALAD

This is a gorgeous and delicious salad: sweet, tart, crisp, soft, green, orange, and purple — an absolute delight to the eye and palate.

For the salad:
- 3 cups (711 ml) baby lettuce mix, washed and dried
- 2 fresh peaches
- 1 starfruit
- A handful of pansies

For the dressing:
- ¾ cup (177 ml) extra-virgin olive oil
- ½ teaspoon (2.5 ml) salt
- ½ teaspoon (2.5 ml) paprika
- ⅓ cup (79 ml) honey
- ¼ teaspoon (1.3 ml) mustard
- ¼ teaspoon (1.3 ml) freshly ground black pepper
- ¼ cup (59 ml) lemon juice

Making the Salad

1. Divide the lettuce among four serving plates. Cut the peaches in half around the pit and twist the halves apart. Remove the pit; slice each peach half into four sections. Cut the starfruit into slices.

2. Divide the peaches and starfruit among the four salads.

Making the Dressing

1. Mix all the ingredients in a jar. Cover and shake until blended.

2. Drizzle the dressing over the salads. Just before serving, sprinkle the pansies over the salads.

MAKES 4 SERVINGS

CHILDREN'S VIOLET GRAPE PARTY MOLD

In the 1950s, Jell-O molds were all the rage. Today Jell-O is no longer considered upscale party fare, even though lots of adults and children love it. But this fruit-filled mold, topped with violets, is pretty enough for any party! It's not hard to make, but it does take some time and patience.

1 package (3 ounces) lemon-flavored gelatin
2 cups (473 ml) boiling water, divided
5 violets
¾ cup (177 ml) white grape juice
1 cup (237 ml) seedless white grapes, halved
1 package (3 ounces) grape-flavored gelatin
¾ cup (177 ml) cold water
1 cup (237 ml) seedless purple grapes, halved
Grape leaves and additional violets for decoration
   (optional)

1. Place the lemon-flavored gelatin in a bowl. Pour 1 cup (237 ml) of boiling water over the gelatin; mix well. Pour a little of the gelatin into a 4-cup (946 ml) mold, so it just covers the bottom. Place the violets upside down in the gelatin, making sure the flowers are partially covered with gelatin. Chill the mold until the gelatin is set but not yet firm.

2. Meanwhile, stir the grape juice into the remaining lemon gelatin. Chill until the mixture is the consistency of unbeaten egg whites. Stir in the white grapes. Pour this mixture over the violet layer. Chill until set but not firm.

3. Place the grape-flavored gelatin in a bowl. Pour 1 cup (237 ml) of boiling water over the gelatin; mix well. Add ¾ cup (177 ml) of cold water and mix. Chill until the mixture is the consistency of unbeaten egg whites. Stir in the purple grapes. Pour this mixture over the white grape layer. Chill until firm.

4. Unmold the dessert onto a serving platter. Decorate the edges with grape leaves and violets if desired.

MAKES 8 SERVINGS

PANSY PEAR PANCAKES

This is a pretty pancake for a special breakfast. The flowers will fade a little during cooking, and you won't want the pancakes to brown too much, so don't make these in a cast-iron skillet and don't let the pan get too hot.

1   cup (237 ml) flour
1   tablespoon (15 ml) light brown sugar
2   teaspoons (30 ml) baking powder
¼   teaspoon (1.3 ml) salt
1   cup (237 ml) vanilla yogurt
1   tablespoon (15 ml) safflower oil
1   egg
1   tablespoon (15 ml) water
¼   cup (59 ml) finely diced pears
2   tablespoons (30 ml) butter
9   pansies
Wildflower honey, brown sugar, or maple syrup

1. Sift together the flour, brown sugar, baking powder, and salt into a bowl. In another bowl, combine the yogurt, oil, egg, and water; whisk until well blended. Add the pears; mix well.

2. Pour the wet ingredients into the flour mixture and stir until just combined.

3. Heat a frying pan or griddle over medium. Add a little butter; heat until melted. Pour a scant ¼ cup (59 ml) of batter into the pan for each pancake. Gently press a pansy, face up, into the center of each pancake. Cook until the edges of the pancake are dry; turn and cook briefly on the other side.

4. Serve the pancakes flower side up with honey, brown sugar, or syrup.

Makes 4 servings

Other Storey Titles You Will Enjoy

The Flower Gardener's Bible, by Lewis and Nancy Hill.
All the advice you need on flower gardening, from
the basics of plant care to inspiration for theme gardens.
384 pages. Paper. ISBN 978-1-58017-462-6.
Hardcover. ISBN 978-1-58017-463-3.

*The Gardener's A–Z Guide to Growing Flowers from
Seed to Bloom,* by Eileen Powell.
An encyclopedic reference on choosing, sowing, transplanting,
and caring for 576 annuals, perennials, and bulbs.
528 pages. Paper. ISBN 978-1-58017-517-3.

Herb Mixtures & Spicy Blends, by Maggie Oster.
More than 100 flavorful recipes gathered from
herb shops and farms across North America.
160 pages. Paper. ISBN 978-0-88266-918-2.

Herbal Teas, by Kathleen Brown.
A collection of blends to brew your own soothing,
invigorating, healthy, or just plain delicious teas.
160 pages. Paper. ISBN 978-1-58017-099-4.

Herbal Vinegar, by Maggie Oster.
Dozens of recipes for vinegars that put herbs,
spices, vegetables, and flowers to flavorful use.
176 pages. Paper. ISBN 978-0-88266-843-7.

Serving Up the Harvest, by Andrea Chesman.
A collection of 175 recipes to bring out the best in garden-fresh
vegetables, with 14 master recipes that can accommodate
whatever happens to be in your produce basket.
516 pages. Paper. ISBN 978-1-58017-663-7.

These and other books from Storey Publishing are available
wherever quality books are sold or by calling 1-800-441-5700.
Visit us at *www.storey.com.*